AF444513

THE PERFECT
Petal

The Perfect Petal

Copyright © 2024 Millicent R. Baker
All rights reserved.

This is a work of fiction. Names, characters, places, and incidents either are the product of the authors' imagination or are used fictitiously. Any resemblance to actual persons, living or dead, events, or locales is entirely coincidental.

No parts of this book may be reproduced in any form or by any electronic or mechanical means, including information storage in retrieval systems, without written permission from the authors, except in the case of a reviewer, who may quote brief passages embodied in critical articles or in a review.

ISBN:

Editor: Crystal S. Wright

10 9 8 7 6 5 4 3 2 1

Printed in the United States

Priceless Publishing®
pricelesspublishing.co

Is Love Real...

Contents

I

Intro

1

Chapter 1

Karrington + Dominique

11

Chapter 2

Who is Dominique McCullin?

24

Chapter 3

How It Started...

How It's Going 3 Months Later...

29

Chapter 4

Decisions Have To Be Made

43

Chapter 5

The Perfect Petal

62

About The Author

63

Stay In Touch

Intro

Karrington and Dominique have had a great first date. Because they are coworkers, they are both concerned about how work will look after their passionate night out. Other than navigating her fantasies, Karrington and her friends have really evolved. Lillian is married with a daughter, Morgan is thriving as a nurse in California, and Gabby is finding herself and is ready to find love. Karrington and Dominique are trying to make their relationship work along without jeopardizing their jobs or careers.

CHAPTER 1

Karrington + Dominique

DATE NIGHT CONCLUDES...

Karrington and Dominique have just had an amazing evening where they discovered aspects of themselves that they'd never known.

Karrington had no idea the intense longing that was lying dormant within her...until now. The night gave her a fulfillment that she had never known. *It's like I can see colors now after living in a black-and-white world*, she thought. But she's a professional first and about her business. So, after Dominique leaves and she's out of the shower, she gets ready for her first day on this new project as the thoughts of Dominique help her fall asleep.

After hearing Karrington lock the door, Dominique slowly turns and walks to his car. He looks up while backing out of her driveway and catches a glimpse of her undoing her ponytail through the window. He can't help but let the night play on repeat in his mind for a minute. Dominique has not been here before. He has been so careful, for so long, but tonight made him realize what he has been missing.

He snaps back to reality when her lights go off. He realizes that he needs to get home to prepare his mind for tomorrow which is a few hours away. Before he knew it, Dominique was home. His thoughts of Karrington got him there in record time. *Not only is tomorrow a work day but it's an important day that will include Karrington. I'm going to have to put these feelings somewhere.* Dominique knows that she should be there, as she is an amazing attorney, but he also knows she is an amazing lover. *Man, I've never been here before. I don't know how tomorrow is going to go, but Dominique, you've got to pull yourself together, man.*

Hoping to wash away the intrusive thoughts, Dominique goes to take a shower. He calls Karrington to say good night, but she doesn't answer.

THE NEXT DAY—KARRINGTON'S MORNING
Karrington wakes up from the sound of her obnoxious alarm clock. Usually, she would snooze but today was different, the outfit she chose is no longer good enough. *I don't know what I need to wear, but I can't wear anything like that!* Karrington stares at her black dress from the night before and she realizes today is a new day. *Today is a professional day even though I can still feel this man inside of me I have got to focus.*

After Karrington left Jonathan, she promised herself she would never let a man interrupt her life. No matter how good *it* or he was, and after the night they had, she had to prove her willingness to be submissive was not to be confused with her formidable performance in the courtroom. *I hope Dominque is ready,* she whispered to herself as she continued to prepare for the day.

She turns on some music and calls her parents like she always does before she starts anything. Karrington decided to wear a dark grey suit with a white blouse. She puts on her signature red lip and her brown hair perfectly falls in place. As she changes her bag, her blindfold falls on the floor and her thoughts are all over the place, then her phone rings...

DOMINQUE'S MORNING

Dominque finally wakes up and Karrington is the first thought he has as he sits on the side of his bed and thinks about last night and how important today is.

As his thoughts are solely on Karrington, he knows this is the case of a lifetime. *"I am going to have to rewrite the policy and procedures as it pertains to relationships in the workplace,"* He pushes himself up and prepares for the day. *How is this meeting going to go? My position is the focal point now. I have a job to do.* For the first time in his professional life, he is unsure.

Dominique is never visually disappointing, he puts on his grey slacks, and crisp white button-down and finishes the look with the perfect Windsor knot, that he is known for, in his tie. He grabs his coffee from the counter, throws his coat over his arms, and continues out of the door. Dominique is steady and sound when he speaks with his team, but today along with this big drug case, he is anticipating his obsession — Karrington. He decides to call her to say good morning. They end up talking to each other while making their way to work.

"Good morning, Pretty Girl." Dominique could no longer call Karrington "Kid" and he realized too late that "Pretty Girl" may not work either.

"Good morning, Dom. As much as I love being your Pretty Girl, we're going to have to refrain from that."

His smile seemed to disappear but he was also relieved. Her transparency made him respect her even more.

Karrington continued. *"I am an attorney first and I am here for myself. I have so much respect for you and who you are. I would not want to blur those lines. So just 'Karrington' or 'Kay' is fine. You can debrief with your 'Pretty Girl' later tonight."*

Dominique could hear Karrington's smile, and he respected her so much at that moment. With a laugh, he says, *"Okay, Karri, I can do that. I look forward to debriefing later, now that I know that's a thing."* He goes on to fill her in on some specifics of the case. Karrington and Dominique have a conversation that seems foreign compared to last night. They are two different people who are good at what they do. Karrington has a lot to prove to Dominique when it comes to being an attorney, she doesn't want him to see her as his submissive lover until it's time for that.

TIME TO WORK

Dominique and Karrington hung up and continued to work. Dominique is excited. He will see Karrington soon. He's focused and expecting a favorable outcome. Dominique loves working with his team, and it seems like he's going to end his day with Karrington. Then a smile just rolls across his face when he sees Karrington in the parking lot. He parks in his space and gets out of the car, reaches for his coat and when he turns around, Karrington is there.

"What's up twin!" she says.

 That broke the ice. They are both wearing grey suits. They laugh and walk into the building together as colleagues.

Dominique says turning to her. *"I can't wait to hear what you have today."*

Karrington smiled and she released a sigh of relief because she lives for the law.

Karrington walked into the boardroom with the team. She was awestruck as she began to take in her real first day on the job. Everyone was professional and cool. There were people taking coffee and lunch orders for the team. Even the seating was strategic. Dominique sits in the middle of the table and the team branches out on both sides according to specialty or seniority. Karrington had a 2nd seat which is surprising and perfect. She feels seen and respected as an attorney.

After Dominique finishes addressing the team, he turns to Karrington and says, *"Karrington is new to the team but I wanted her on this case because of her experience. She has a winning track record on cases like these."*

Karrington didn't know if this was because of how she took him in last night or what, but she was about to take her moment.

After the morning brief was over and all parties had their assignments, Karrington was a little apprehensive at first, but quickly realized that this was a real team. After her meeting with the lead investigator, she had gone to her office to eat her lunch and continue her work as the day was coming to an end. While she is reading over everything from the day, her phone buzzes. Picking it up, she sees a text from 'Daddy' which is the name she has given Dominique in her phone. She wasn't quite sure if she knew how to process it while in work mode, but she opened it anyway. It said:

> *Today has been one of the best days in this office because of you, I am so happy you decided to work on this team and I hope you are comfortable and you are truly an asset to this office. I realize we are at work, but I want to look at you and watch pleasure come over your face as I navigate to your wetness and bring you to climax, but we can debrief later.*

Karrington didn't know how to take the text. Although she was turned on and ready to debrief, she realized that Dominique didn't understand what she meant from their conversation this morning, but she responded with a smiley face emoji and the words, *"Can't wait."* Karrington started to gather her things and prepare to leave for the day. As people are on their way out, they stop to say goodbye and how great her proposal was today. This made Karrington feel confident and happy about her move to start over, but at that moment, she thought about what Gabby had said to her, *"Friend, please take this slow. You go so deep, so fast."*

Karrington knows that her friend is right, and she knows this about herself. Karrington is making the changes that she needs, but she sees that Mr. McCullin is walking to his car and it's time to debrief. Karrington laughs to herself. *I'm setting boundaries, but it's time to debrief and I'm not going to set them all today.* She laughs and shakes her head because she knows she is a mess and leaves her office. When she gets to her car, she can hear a car pulling up, it's Dominique.

He slows down and puts his window down. *"Awesome job today, Karri. I do want to apologize for the text. That was a lot, especially at work."*

As she has in the past, Karrington almost makes an excuse for Dominique's less-than-professional behavior but remembers that she is setting boundaries. *"It was a lot. Dom and I would appreciate it if that never happened again. Now, what time are you coming over?"*

Dominique nods in agreement and tells Karrington he will see her later. He spoke in a very low tone in case anyone was listening. They decided to stay at Dominique's as he's closer to work.

Karrington went home and packed a bag for the night. She decided to call Lillian because she didn't want to hear a sermon from Gabby. Karrington told Lillian about her day and let her know she was about to go to Dominique's, the ladies laughed and caught up with each other. When Karrington hung up the phone she grabbed her bag, turned off her lights, and headed out to engage in bad behavior.

DEBRIEF NIGHT

Karrington texted Dominique for directions to his place and learned they didn't live that far apart. *I know I should not be on my way over there, but I'm new here and he's fun, but I must stay in control.* Karrington was trying to make sense of her decision to go to Dominique's. She feels like she already knows the outcome, but she continues to drive to the debriefing. She also doesn't know what this night is going to bring because the last night they were together was a little different.

Dominique was excited about seeing Karrington in a more relaxed environment, he realized he may have crossed the line with Karrington at work and he was going to do some shifting. He had to let that go because this night is just two individuals who enjoy each other and it's going to be different than the last interaction.

Karrington arrives and Dominique greets her at the door. They both were very visually comfortable. Dominique could not help looking at Karrington in what he feels is her most beautiful state. She had on a pair of grey yoga pants, what looked like her favorite worn AKA pullover, no makeup, and her hair was in a bun. Dominique quickly met her and reached for her bag. Dominique's build is identifiable with anything he's wearing. Like Dominique, Karrington found him to be less intimidating, which made her more comfortable. His black Nike sweatpants and a white t-shirt laying on his chiseled body made Karrington exhale. "Come on in Pretty Girl, I ordered your appetizers, and I got the champagne you like," Karrington smiled and took his hand as he led her into the house.

The night was very normal. Dominique was taking Karrington's lead, he wanted her to feel comfortable and their conversation was different, smart, funny, and insightful. Karrington learned that she and Dominique grew up in similar environments, they were exceptional because of their environment, and they both felt better about being right in front of each other at this moment. Karrington asks if she could kiss him, and the Veuve Clicquot is kicking in. Dominique smiles and asks, "Are we trading places tonight?" Karrington only smiles and props herself up on her knees leans in and says, *"Nope I just wanted a kiss. I'm sure you have something planned. A room you'd like to show me or maybe some items you'd like to use, I don't know."*

After Karrington gets her kiss, Dominique says, *"Not any of that, we started out pretty fast. I want to slow it down and see what we build up to."*

Karrington sat back and looked at him, she nodded and said, *"Okay. You have my attention."*

Dominique told her he would be right back, and he disappeared into what Karrington assumed was his bedroom.

She could hear water running and him just moving around. From her initial interaction with Dom, she doesn't know where he could go, but she's focusing on the slow down and how the evening will go.

Dominique walked back out with that smile that caused Karrington to throb and he knew he had her undivided attention. *"Come here."* Dominique's voice was soft and stern and this caused Karrington to leap off of the couch. Once she was in front of him, he took her hand and led her into the room. Karrington was curious but she felt safe with her guy. The room smelled like cinnamon and she could see the bathroom was dimly lit.

Dominique turned to look at Karrington and he smiled and began to speak. *"Karri, you are so beautiful. Tonight I just want to take care of you."*

Karrington was quiet and attentive as he continued.

"I will let you know every step. First, let me undress you."

Karrington stood still and her body obeyed Dominique's every touch. He raised her sweatshirt over her head exposing her pink lace bra and he awarded her with kisses on her cheeks. Next, he kneeled to pull her tights down and kissed her thighs on the way back up. Dominique stood silently to take Karrington in with his eyes before he pulled her close to passionately kiss her. Pulling his lips from hers, he took her hand and led her into the bathroom.

When she entered the bathroom, she gasped in surprise. There were candles everywhere and a subtle but provocative cinnamon aroma in the air. Rose petals were floating on top of the water. She looked at him and smiled as she stood on her tiptoes for a kiss.

"Let me help you in and I'll get you a drink," Dominique offered.

Karrington watched Dominique until he disappeared from her sight. She leaned back to enjoy her warm bath. She didn't know that she needed this but somehow Dominique did. She was so relaxed that she didn't realize the moment that he returned. When she opened her eyes, he was there with her drink in one hand and a chair in the other.

"What are you doing with that chair? You're not getting in?" Karrington asked.

Dominique didn't speak at first, he handed Karrington her drink and positioned himself right in front of her. Her face was soft from the candlelight as he gazed at her until he finally spoke.

"I'm going to bathe you and take care of you tonight."

—————————

They laughed and talked about everything from work to school and even their most recent favorite restaurants. Dominique finally got up and kneeled by the tub, his hands slowly entered the warm water to explore Karrington's body.

He could tell he'd found the right spot by the way her back arched. He continued to explore. Their eyes were locked together as Karrington made a splash of her own. Dominique left to retrieve a towel. He helped her out of the bath, wrapped her in the towel, and carried her to his bed where he sat her down gently.

The candlelight in the bedroom softened Dominique's face and Karrington couldn't take her eyes off of him as she felt him navigating over her moist body with tenderness and care. There was no audience tonight, no blindfold, and no surprises — just two people who wanted to please and be pleased. There was no music other than the sounds of pleasure from two people who were learning each other. She couldn't imagine how many more times Dominique was going to bring her to her peak and forbid her to release. After what seemed like hours, Karrington was visibly trembling. When would he allow her to have her climax?

As if reading her mind, at that very moment he nibbled her ear and said, *"Give it to me."*

As Karrington exhaled her entire being she managed to whisper, *"Who are you, Dominique McCullin?!"*

CHAPTER 2

Who is Domonique McCullin?

Dominique Eli McCullin is not just the top attorney in West Virginia. He's in a class of his own. Growing up in Liberty, Pennsylvania, he had to work harder than the ones who got the most by doing the least. He became socially skilled growing up in Liberty. Dominique is exceptional in every way.

Dominique's father, Eli, was a school principal. This was his first example of a hardworking, responsible man. His mother, Jewel, was a nurse and his role model for how to treat people. He has two sisters and a brother, all successful. Dominique and his siblings are close, they speak often, and they support each other in all endeavors. Their parents raised them to look out for each other. It was just understood growing up in Liberty where they were the minority. Luckily, they never had problems and the community loved the McCullin kids.

Being the oldest, Dominique is very protective of his siblings and even his friends. He has always been described as very loyal and a great person to be around. Excellence just came naturally to him. He never had to study hard, this allowed him to be well-rounded without his grades being negatively impacted. He played basketball, served as the president of the National Honor Society, and graduated at the top of his high school class as the valedictorian. People found him to be exceptional but despite this, he was very responsible and respectful.

Growing up in Liberty, he had friends of all races, but his dad would always caution him that he could not do what "ALL" his friends did. An incident that happened to Dominique's friend, Kendrick, made his father's words ring true. Dominique and his best friend, Kendrick Pryor, had known each other since kindergarten until they became stars on their high school basketball team. Dominique lost Kendrick to an unfortunate police incident that neither he nor the team was present for.

The team had been scheduled for a playoff game and they were supposed to meet at the school. Kendrick left early to pick up something for his trip and planned to meet up with the team afterward. Kendrick was on his way to his car when police officers who were patrolling the area pulled up and asked where he was going. Understanding the environment, Kendrick complied and told the officer where he was going. The officer got out of his car and continued to question Kendrick who was forthcoming. The officer got angrier for no apparent reason. He pulled out his handcuffs and Kendrick finally asked him a question, *"Sir, why am I being arrested? I have a playoff game to get to and I didn't do anything."* This infuriated the officer who began to choke Kendrick until he was no longer breathing.

When Kendrick didn't show, Dominique knew exactly where he was. He and his teammates left to go to the store around the corner. As they were pulling up, they saw the officer with his hands around Kendrick's throat. What Dominique didn't know was that his friend had stopped breathing at that moment. Almost like he held on till his friends became witnesses to the tragedy. As Dominique began to question the police officer about what happened, he was approached aggressively and told to stay in his place. He realized that the only thing that saved him was the presence of his white friend, Tim Allen, who the officer asked to leave and take Dominique with him.

Dominique wasn't going to leave the scene before informing his friend's parents of what had transpired. When his friend's parents arrived, Dominique witnessed how the police dishonestly explained why their son wouldn't ever come home. At that moment, Dominique wanted justice for his friend. Sometime later, due to traffic camera footage that recorded the incident, the police officer was found guilty.

Dominique knew that he wanted to protect the innocent and put away individuals who used their authority to intimidate and sometimes lead to the death of others. He decided he was going to become a lawyer. The death of his friend has been the foundation and driving force of his career.

Dominique continued to be responsible and respectful in every aspect of his life, but he learned other things about himself when it came to his dating life.

DOMINIQUE THE DOMINANT

Dominique McCullin is a very patient, respectful, and controlled man. He developed those traits from life experiences. He attended Bowie State, an HBCU is exactly the puzzle piece he needed to shape his future. He was very focused in school, driven by the death of his friend, Kendrick. This fueled him in college to be the best political science major he could be. Though he didn't play basketball competitively in college, he spent time in the gym and on the court daily. But as serious as he was about academics, he found time to enjoy himself.

He is extraordinary in dating as well, and in college, he discovered that he was a bit more adventurous than most men. He was always a very handsome man and this brought the ladies around. Dominique has much respect for women which led him to be exclusive when dating. He had a couple of relationships in college but one changed him forever.

Dominique met Neely Vaughan during the Fall of their second year at Bowie State. She was in one of his classes and they were paired for assignments. He was smitten. Eventually, Dominique asked her out and they became inseparable. Dominique and Neely were the perfect match. When they returned to school after the Christmas holiday, he decided to take it to the next level. They had discussed being together over the holidays so he knew that Neely was on board.

Dominique had secretly saved money from his holiday job to plan the perfect night with Neely when they returned to school. He called the local Marriott and reserved the presidential suite. They both had crossed last spring so he had the room decorated in her sorority colors using pink roses and green accents. He left Liberty a little early so he could pick her up from the airport. She was coming in from South Carolina and he wanted to be there when she landed.

While driving together from the airport, they talked about their holiday and made plans to exchange in the room. Dominque disclosed that he had made reservations for them to have dinner before heading to the hotel. Hearing this, Neely smiled and put her hand on his thigh as they drove the rest of the way in silence. Up until that point they had kissed and fooled around but tonight is the night they would go all the way.

Neely was astonished by the intentional décor in the suite. She could see how much effort Dominique had put in for their special night. She wrapped her arms around him and gave him a loving kiss that led them to the shower. They showered together and then dried each other off. Dominique guided her to the room asking was she ready, Neely whispered, *"Yes."*

Neely felt handled and not in a gentle way. Dominique became aggressive though not hurtful. She was confused because he was usually so gentle and careful. She looked up at him and his calm expression was out of touch with his aggressive movements. Neely asked him to stop.

"Dominique, you are hurting me. Can we slow down," she said softly.

Dominique immediately moved away and apologized profusely. *"I am so sorry, Neely. That's not my intention!"*

Dominique was not trying to hurt Neely. He thought he was pleasing her. Quickly scanning her body with his eyes, he saw that her neck was red where his hands had been. Appalled at himself, he moved further away from her. He told her that they could just lie there and talk.

But Neely was in the mood, and she didn't believe that he meant to hurt her. She looked at him, *"Dominique, I got you. Let me get up top and we can ride into the night."*

Neely straddled him. Though they enjoyed each other, Dominique didn't let her know that this was not as romantic to him. Something was off about her being in control. Nonetheless, he and Neely finished beautifully and fell asleep.

Their relationship continued into their junior year but Neely is focused. Although she's happy with Dominique, her education and career are her priorities. When they returned for their last year at Bowie State it was going to be imperative to study hard and stay focused. Neely communicated to Dominique that the upcoming final year requires her full attention. Dominique understood as they were scheduled to take some of the same rigorous courses in the Fall. It was time to focus on finishing strong.

They were accepted into two of the same law schools, excited to be accepted to the schools they applied to. Dominique chose Georgetown in D.C. and Neely chose the University of South Carolina School of Law as it is closer to home for her in Columbia. Dominique and Neely could talk about anything, and he loved that about their relationship. They went out the last night before summer vacation. When it was time for the night to end, Neely asked him to take her back to her place so she could go out with her sorors one last time.

The next day Dominique picked Neely up to take her to the airport. While en route to the airport his frat brother and best friend, Colin, called. Hearing the stress in his voice Dominique asked, *"What's up frat? What's going on?"*

Dominique could hear the hesitation in his voice. Colin lowered his voice. *"Frat, are you with Neely? If you are, don't let her know that I'm asking about her."*

Curious but cautious, Dominique postponed the call. He told Colin that he'd call him as soon as he dropped Neely off and they hung up.

Neely noticed that Dominique looked stressed after the short call. *"Dom, is everything okay?"*

Dominique pulled up to her terminal and responded, *"I'll call him later."* With that, he got out of the car to get Neely's bags. Finally, he opened her door. *"Come give me a hug."*

Neely got on her tiptoes like she had to each time she hugged and kissed him. *"I'll text when I land and call you later."*

"Okay," Dominique replied. He watched Neely until she disappeared into the crowd. He got back in his car and drove off.

As Dominique got on Hwy 170, he called Colin. Colin Brooks has a very strong personality. He stands about six feet tall and has a hazel gaze that would make you melt. He and Dominique met freshman year when they were roommates and they have been best friends ever since. They were like brothers, and they looked out for each other.

"Hey frat," Dominique said when Colin picked up. *"What was all that about? Why couldn't you talk to me with Neely in the car?"*

Colin didn't want to have this conversation but he knew he had to. *"Frat, were you with Neely last night?"*

Dominique answered in the affirmative and kept listening. *"What's going on, Colin?"*

Colin took a deep, shaky breath. *"So, after Neely left you last night, she went to her soror's place. They had a party. She showed up with another guy. My girl and I were there and when we saw her, we were looking for you. I was on my way towards her when I saw a guy behind her. I kind of moved away quickly so she couldn't see me. Ashtiny was there with her friends. She could hear the conversation Neely was having with her sorors. Their nosiness paid off this time. Knowing how close you and I are, Ash told me what she heard Neely saying."*

Feeling his hands begin to shake, Dominique pulled over as Colin continued.

"Apparently Neely told her line sisters that you are nice but there is something wrong with you."

Dominique realized at that moment why Neely said she would text him. She didn't want to talk to him if he found out what she said or who she was with.

Colin continued softly. *"She said you have weird sexual ways and want to do things she doesn't want to do. Then she went on to basically say that y'all have just been friends this semester and that she has been sleeping with someone else."*

Dominique started driving again and remained silent. He knew Colin was trying to break this to him nicely cause usually, he is extremely blunt.

Colin continued speaking into the silence. *"Now she didn't say that you did anything to her. Just that you have weird ways."*

Dominique knew exactly what Neely was referring to. He asked Colin to meet him at his place. *"I'll be there soon."*

Colin said, *"Bet,"* and they hung up.

When he got home, Dominique poured himself a drink and sat in his disbelief. Colin's knock on the door brought him back to reality. He yelled to Colin to come in. Colin could tell that Dominque was upset about the news he had given him earlier. He sat down quietly.

Dominique told him everything. Dominque's heart was broken. Colin's broke a little when Dominque asked, *"Man, what's wrong with me? I love Neely and I have nothing but respect for her. That's why I didn't push her. I wanted her to be comfortable."*

Colin answered only like he could. *"At the end of the day, she's not about to have you smoking out the window, frat. She knew she was wrong. You know me, frat. I'm going to be here for you."* Colin is a little rough around the edges but that's why they are so close. *"My girl told me about it and she also told me there was a girl who wants to meet you. See, you're up already!"*

Colin was finally able to make Dominique smile. *"Frat, I need a minute."*

Colin understood and told him he'd pick him up for a game tomorrow and left.

Dominique locked the door and got into bed, still hurt. He could not believe that Neely would speak about him like that. They had the same goals and had discussed the life they wanted. He loved her and believed she was the one for him.

After a couple of hours, he received a text from Neely. She said that she had made it and that she'd call him later. Dominique didn't know what to say. He stared at the text for a couple of minutes. Finally, he texted back, *"Glad you made it. Have a good summer."* He was hoping that his message would make it clear that he didn't want to talk to her this summer or any other summer, fall, winter, or spring. He understood and accepted that Neely didn't want him but held out hope that there was someone in the world for him.

THE DOMINANT IS BORN

Dominique was not interested at the time in whoever Colin was trying to set him up with. He was focused on his part-time job and working on his packet for law school. But a couple of weeks into the summer, he decided it was time to have a little fun, so he decided to call Colin.

"What up, frat?" Colin answered.

Dominique cut to the chase. *"Man, I am giving you a call to ask about the girl you were telling me about some weeks ago."*

Colin thought about it for a second before replying. *"Oh, you mean the girl I told you that Ashtiny knew? Hold on, Ashtiny's here. I'll let her tell you about her friend."* Colin called out to Ashtiny in the kitchen.

"What's up, babe?" Ashtiny said, entering the room. She is breathtaking. Her long black hair frames her caramel-colored face and falls to her shoulders. She's southern and you can tell from how she speaks. She and Colin have been together since sophomore year and he lingers on each word she speaks.

"What's your girl's name again? The one that you were with the night we were at the party. Dom may want to go out with her," Colin said.

"Oh Dom," Ashtiny said happily. She didn't need the phone because Dominique could hear her just fine. *"Her name is Tameca Myles and she is so cool! I think you two would really hit it off and have a lot in common. I'm 'bout to go call her and set up a double date."* Turning to her boo she asked, *"Is that good with you, babe?"*

Colin replied, *"Just let me know, baby."*

With that, Ashtiny went to call Tameca. Colin and Dominique realized they would see each other soon so they said their goodbyes and hung up.

Dominique got word from Colin that they were on for the following night. That was okay with Dominique because he needed to get out. What he didn't know was that this date would change his life forever.

. . . .

Dominique showed up at Jerry's Seafood to meet up with Colin and Ashtiny, as they were all feigning for crab. Shortly after he got there and secured their table he heard Colin's deep scratchy voice. *"What's up, frat."*

They locked up to greet each other. Dominique greeted Ashtiny with a kiss on the cheek and then realized it was just the three of them. Seeing the worried look on his face, Ashtiny reassured him that Tameca was right behind them.

Shortly after that, she arrived and he was in awe. Dominique thought she looked like an angel. He looked at Ashtiny and whispered, *"She's beautiful."*

Ashtiny smiled and introduced them. *"Dominique, this is Tameca. Tameca, I'd like you to meet Dominique."*

Tameca reached out her hand. *"Hello Dominique,"* she said, flashing a shy smile that lit up her face. Her copper-colored hair was perfectly swooped across her forehead into the most perfect bob. *"I hope you approve."*

"I do," was his reply. Dominique was smitten immediately.

The group sat down and engaged in small talk. Dominique and Tameca laughed and learned about each other. After dinner, Tameca asked if he would like to go get a drink with her at Tabu, a bar that is open late. Dominique agreed. He'd been in this area for 3 years and had never heard of the place but he was excited. Colin and Ashtiny smiled and looked on with approval. Tameca asked if he wanted to ride with her and he said yes. Colin decided to drive Domonique's car to his house and have Ashtiny drive him. They said their goodbyes and everyone was off.

Domonique felt that Tameca was perfect. They talked until they made it to Tabu. She took his mind off Neely completely.

A few minutes later, Tameca pulled up to a beautiful building. She turned the car off and turned to Dominique. Looking at him intentionally she said, *"I was with Ashtiny that night. I heard what Neely said about you and I knew I had to meet you, not so much for myself, but for you."*

Dominique's forehead wrinkled in confusion. *"What are you talking about? What do you mean 'for me'?"*

Softly, she told him to come and open her door. Dominique followed her instructions. This was not what he was used to but surprisingly, he was a little turned on by this small, five-foot woman making commands. Tameca gracefully swung her legs out of the car. She took his hand and they walked toward the Tabu entrance.

When they went in, the look on Dominique's face was a mixture of satisfaction and relief. He asked, *"Tameca, what is this place?"*

She turned and looked at him. *"Your playground. This is where you belong."*

Dominique had never been to a BDSM club before and he felt ironically comfortable. Tameca held his hand and led him through the dimly lit red rooms. They stopped in a room where they could watch other couples enjoy each other. Releasing his hand, Tameca closed the door behind them. She walked toward Dominique.

Stopping in front of him, she rose on the tip of her toes and uttered words Dominique didn't know he needed to hear till they touched his ear. *"I'm here to please you."*

Dominique felt his body release all tension with this invitation and permission to be himself. He could feel himself becoming erect. Whispering, he told Tameca to undress. He wanted to see her. She obeyed. Dominique watched her, captivated.

Sensing his reluctance, Tameca whispered, *"I will obey you, Sir."*

He talked to Tameca quietly as the couples they watched stimulated him. Dominique felt comfortable and in control. To see her follow his directions pleased him. He now knew that there were women who enjoyed the same sexual experiences as he did. He and Tameca were wrapped up in each other for hours and she fulfilled his every need.

They lay together, relaxing. When it was time to leave, she said, *"I wanted to make sure you knew that there is nothing wrong with you. You are a special man so it will take a special woman to satisfy you and make you happy."*

When they got to the car, Dominique opened her door. He said he'd drive to his place. As they drove, she assured him again that he was exceptional. Tameca made it clear that this was not the start of a relationship. She goes on to explain that she remembers how it feels to be confused about sexual desires, not knowing what to do.

Oddly, Dominique understood exactly what she meant and he appreciated her. When they arrived at his place, they both got out so Tameca could get in the driver's seat. Dominique was standing a bit taller than he was when he left home hours before. He was more confident than ever. Dominique was willing to wait on his special woman. Bending down, he kissed Tameca on the cheek and said, *"I'd like to thank you for what you've done. I don't want you to feel taken advantage of. You have changed my life."*

Tameca kissed his cheek and replied, *"Dominique we will be friends forever. You can call me if you need a ride…in a car."* They laughed and said their goodbyes.

CHAPTER 3

How It Started...How It's Going 3 Months Later...

Dominique's staff worked very hard on the biggest drug case that they've had to date. Not surprisingly, the result was no different than before — they were victorious. Dominique is very proud of his entire team but Karrington was the star. He was in awe of her work ethic. It was her team that pulled the evidence that secured the conviction giving them the win.

Over the last few months, Dominique and Karrington have not spent much time with each other outside of a couple of nights here and there. They are both focused on their work and their priorities were aligned. They could truly respect this about each other and it is why their relationship works as well as it does.

Karrington and her team were responsible for contacting the family who they represented and completing their business. Afterward, it was time to relax, and like Karrington, the entire office, was looking forward to that.

It was typical for Dominique to check in with the staff at the end of each day. She could hear him on his way to her before she saw him.

"Karri, great work. The way you delivered what you found was absolutely beautiful."

She walked towards him and very quietly said, *"I have other beautiful work that I can deliver later tonight."*

Dominique smiled and loosened the Windsor knot in his tie, but he was a little confused, he didn't want to cross the line. He backed up and said, "I don't want to cross your boundaries, I respect your decisions."

Karrington looked at Dominique. *"You're right. I want this to be different."* She apologized and turned to get her things.

Dominique turned and said before he left out of her office, *"When we get outside, I will let you know that I'll bring the tie for your wrists tonight."* Her nod and smile was all he needed.

Dominique gave everyone the following Monday off, other than asking them to check their emails to make sure nothing is missed, this is consistent with how it goes after a win. He also had plans for him and Karrington, so there was an extra incentive to give everyone a day off. They all left in groups, having conversations on the way to their cars.

Sonia, Karrington's assistant, approached her. *"Karrington, congratulations on bringing the win. Let me buy you a drink."* Sonia was standing with a group of colleagues who were hoping Karrington would accept.

Karrington didn't. *"Thank you all so much, but I just want to have a quiet night at home and go to bed early. But I'll treat Tuesday after work."*

Sonia and the others agreed, excited for next Tuesday.

Karrington went home and Dominique went to his weekly brotherhood smoke. He texted her to check if she had made it safely and let her know that he wouldn't be long. For the first time in three months, Karrington was home and did not have to chase a case or be on an hours-long group call. Though she was looking forward to spending time with Dominique, she was happy to have some time to herself before he arrived. She cleaned up her place, talked to her mom and dad, and ordered food for her and Dominique for the weekend.

As Karrington had settled, her phone rang, it was the girls on a group call. Karrington always has time for her girls. Lillian, Gabby, and Morgan calling couldn't make her happier. She had been missing her friends' calls recently.

"Hey, girls!" Lillian's voice is always so full of energy. Karrington admired how Lillian lived by the beat of her own drum. She was smart and social and when it came to love, she loved who she wanted to be. Lillian continues, *"I want to invite you and your honeys to New Orleans. I want you all to be my special guests for the play that I'm putting on and I won't take no for an answer!"*

The girls have never said no to each other, and they were not going to start now. Lillian was calling to see when they would be available because she is rolling the play out around the dates that work for her friends. The plan was set. The ladies will be headed to New Orleans in a month.

Moving on to catching up, Morgan asks, *"Lill, how are Luna and Adam?"*

Lillian lets them know Luna, her 4-year-old daughter, is great. Adam Lovelace, Lillian's husband, is doing well and he is a partner in his firm, so life is good for Lillian. Gabby is dating, her nursing career is through the roof, and she is now teaching. Morgan discloses that she has become a traveling nurse and is preparing for her wedding in LA in the summer. The ladies can't wait to see each other and catch up in person.

Before they hung up, Gabby had to find out what was going on with Karrington. *"So Karrington. Will you be bringing Dominique to New Orleans so we can drill him, unlike the drilling he's doing to you?"*

The ladies laughed and waited for her to answer. *"Yes. Well, I hope. I will mention it to him tonight. We just finished a 3-month-long drug case which we won so tonight we will celebrate. We're good but sometimes I think he's a little "more good" than me. You know me, I'm like, 'tomorrow, I'm not promised to anyone.'"*

Lillian chimed in because she could see where this was going, *"Y'all, I have to go and we can talk about this later, Luna and Adam are waiting for me for dinner."*

The ladies said their 'love you's' and hung up. Karrington was glad Lillian chimed in because she was not in that mood tonight. She was in a Dominique mood tonight. When she hung up, she noticed Dominique had texted to say that he was on the way. Perfect! Karrington felt accomplished. She's checked in with everyone and now she is ready for whatever adventure Dominique has in mind tonight.

. . . .

When she heard the knock at the door, Karrington almost skipped to open it. She greeted Dominique in what he loved to see her in — her copper-brown hair up in a messy knot, one of his shirts, and a pair of lace panties. When she opens the door and notices the smile that comes across his face, she knows he approves. Dominique walks in wearing his clothes from the office and a subtle smell of cigar smoke. He reached out his arms and swept Karrington off her feet as he placed kisses on her nipples that are now firm. Turning, he skillfully locked the door with one hand and carried her to the bathroom.

He puts her down and starts the shower. They undress each other and meet under the warm stream. Karrington watches mesmerized as the water runs down his chiseled abs. She cannot resist touching him. They exchange steamy kisses and soon, the shower becomes a third party.

Karrington grasps Dominique's rock-hard member and kneels to take him in as the water cascades around her face.

She continues to pleasure him until he says, *"Let me dry you off."* Dominique lifts her and turns off the water.

They step out of the shower and he grabs a towel. Dominique dries himself off, then turns to Karrington. With great attention to detail, he stops each water droplet running over her curves in its tracks. Finally, he gets down to eye-level with her pleasure and buries his face there as Karrington gasps. As he continues to devour her, he instructs her not to release until he tells her to.

Using his tie to secure her wrists, Dominique lays her on the bed. He covers her body with his and slowly enters her. Her passionate moans reassure him that he is where he is supposed to be. They continue to ravish one another until their bodies are limp with satisfaction.

When they gained some strength, Karrington put Jackie Brown on the TV while Dominique fetched their drinks. When he returned to bed, she positioned herself in his arms. It was a perfect fit. Karrington brings up the trip to New Orleans and he gives her his full attention.

Dominique was so excited to finally meet the important women in Karrington's life. *"Of course pretty girl, whatever you want. Let's coordinate our calendars."* They must be discreet in the office when it comes to their relationship.

Karrington was happy and ready for her friends to meet Dominique. She kissed him before falling asleep in his arms.

CHAPTER 4

Decisions Have To Be Made

Karrington is enjoying her Saturday and she is in a positive productive mental space. She's been through alot. Her work is exceptional and she is now the lead for her group. Her family is doing great. Her sister and brother come to Morgantown more often since their parents are getting older. She's able to see them whenever they are home and they always check on her. They are close. Then, there's Dominique.

Dominique is what Karrington needed after being so broken after her divorce from Jonathan. He had changed her and her view on love and trust in a relationship. After her divorce, she promised herself to never compromise her wants and happiness again. When Dominique appeared in her life it was a welcomed interruption. He showed her a different way to express herself sexually and she felt like a student learning about things she'd never imagined. It didn't hurt that Dominique was the best teacher she's ever had. This moment in time was new and foreign.

Lately, she's been questioning if the "Dominique Effect" is over and evaluating what a life with Dominique would look like. Could there be marriage? Children? What about work? Is this how it's going to be forever? Sneaking around was fun, but what would really happen if their relationship came into question in the office? Did Karrington want this forever? Karrington is not willing to derail her life again no matter how good the relationship is and it is good. Karrington falls back into the mess of sheets and pillows and does what works when she feels overwhelmed — call Gabby.

"Hey, Gabby. Girl, what are you doing?"

Gabby was busy gathering her purse, keys, and air pods. *"Hold on girl., let me get in the car. I'm headed out."*

Karrington holds on till Gabby gets in the car.

"Okay girl, I'm back. What's going on?" Gabby asks. Karrington answers, *"Girl, not much, where are you going?"*

Gabby let her know that she spoke to Lillian and although they will be leaving in a week to go to New Orleans for Lillian's play, she needed to get Luna a gift, her birthday is coming up. *"Wow, Luna will be 5 this month? Where has the time gone? May 14th will be here before we know it!"*

They kept talking about the trip and how excited they were to be together again, but Gabby knew something was wrong. *"So, what is going on with you and Dominique, are you nervous about us meeting him or are you about to cut him off."* Gabby knew Karrington better than anyone and she could hear the sigh from Karrington after she asked her the question.

"I really feel like I'm falling in love with him and you know how he handles me." Gabby had made it to the mall. She was in her parking space, nodding as she listened to Karrington. *"But it's something and I don't know what it is. Although he is still very much "THE MAN" at work, he has seemed to have softened when it comes to us."* Gabby knew exactly what Karrington meant and one thing about her friend. She cannot be given an inch. *"I don't want him throwing me around, but throw me around."*

Karrington and Gabby laughed. Gabby finally gathered herself and said, *"K, you are just going to have to tell him if you want this to continue because if not, you are going to hurt or damage him and you will be wrong for that."* Gabby is the one the girls call for honesty, accountability, and confirmation. *"Have you started the part where you need your time and then you don't want to be alone all within an hour, you know that Virgo shit you do?"*

Karrington laughed because she knew her friend was right, Gabby continued and Karrington listened.

The friends hung up and Karrington was trying to decide how and when to talk with Dominique or if she needed to or wanted to, she was just in her head. *I am overthinking this, I just need to let him know I want to take it slow but maintain other parts of our relationship, I know he will understand.* Karrington was thinking to herself and the phone rang. It was Dominique. She was happy because she had had a great day but now she wanted to see him. She laughed to herself after she confirmed that he was coming over and hung up. *Virgo shit,* she mumbled, as she obediently picked out a blindfold and a wrist tie to match her underwear.

NEW ORLEANS...
The time has come, and the ladies are arriving in New Orleans for Lillian's play. Lillian has arranged for her friends to be picked up, in style as they had come in. Lillian is really laying it out because she and her friends haven't seen each other in a while. Adam has prepared the outdoor humidor for the guys and their evening, he's excited. This is actually the first time the men have met. Because of the love that they have for their partners and the bond their ladies share, they have no choice but to become fast friends. Adam decides that he and the guys will stay in while the girls go out for the night.

Morgan and Amir were the first to arrive. The newly engaged couple will be getting married this summer and she wanted the girls to meet him and let her know how they felt before the wedding. Amir Westbrook is a plastic surgeon and he and Morgan met at a Medical Conference in Lancaster, CA. Morgan moved back to California after she finished her master's in nursing school. She was looking in her bag as she was waiting for the speaker and when she heard the smooth baritone voice she immediately looked up from her bag and her heart stopped. Amir walked boldly to the podium, he was tall, and his hazel eyes complimented his almond skin. His voice was clear and deep and when he smiled, she knew she had to meet him, not just to know who he was, but she didn't hear a word he said after she saw him on stage.

When the day was over, she walked towards him and to her surprise, the smile that came over his face was for her, he had spotted her in the audience. She said, "Hello, my name is Morgan St. James," she reached her hand out and as he reached out, he said, "Hi Morgan, I'm Amir Westbrook and if it wasn't for you, I wouldn't have gotten through that speech, you are breathtaking. Can I buy you a drink to say thanks?" Morgan is indeed a beautiful woman; she has filled out since she left school, and her curves are more pronounced. Morgan gasped a little and nodded yes as she had the same thought. After the small talk was over, they went to the bar in the hotel, talked for hours, and realized they lived in the same area. They made plans when they returned home. Many phone calls, visits, and dates later, Morgan and Amir have been together a year, and they are looking forward to spending their lives together.

When Gabby and Rico arrived, she was a bit nervous. Gabby knows how Karrington can be, but she is happy, and she knows that's the most important to Karrington and the other girls. Gabby takes her bag from Rico as he pulls it from the carousel and says, *"Baby, are you nervous about meeting my friends?"*

Rico turned to Gabby leaned in and reassured her. *"Baby, you are nervous. Your friends will love me and I already love them because they are your friends. Stop worrying."*

Gabby smiled as he turned to get the rest of the bags, she could see his arms flex as he lifted the bags and placed them in the cart. Rico Williams has made a difference in Gabby's life and as a police officer, he takes good care of her.

They met when he brought a woman in for treatment who had been a victim of domestic violence. At the time, Rico was not aware of what had happened to Gabby, but he was in awe of how attentive and compassionate she was.

He engaged with her when she walked out of the room. *"Hello, I'm Officer Williams and you are?"*

Gabby was busy and Rico lifted her badge. *"Gabrielle..."* Gabby stopped and said, *"Do you need any more information or help? The patient will be admitted. She must stay overnight for observation."*

He explained that he just needed some information for his report. *"I don't usually do this but you are the most beautiful woman I've ever met. I don't want to be disrespectful. Who takes care of you like that? You must be spoken for."*

Gabby gave a little smile. Officer Williams was very handsome. He had a slender medium build. His beard was lined up perfectly and laid on his face and his brown skin was a plus. Gabby finally spoke, "I take care of myself." Before she knew it, she did something that she hadn't done in a while — she began to flirt. *"Who takes protects you, after you protect others all day?"*

That night they exchanged numbers. Although Gabby was flirty, she was still careful. His being a police officer didn't make a difference. She took her time and Rico was very patient with her. They talked for months. When she felt comfortable, Gabby divulged what happened to her in college. Rico promised he would protect and serve on and off the job when it came to her. Fast forward to the present day, it has been two years. This is the best relationship that she's ever been in.

Rico takes care of her. When she was worried about him being on the street and voiced her concern, he told her he would take it under consideration. Recalling his psychology degree, he applied the next day for the victim advocate position. He knew what his intentions were with Gabby, but he didn't want to get her excited if he wasn't able to get the position.

Rico put all the bags on the cart, and they headed to the car that Lillian sent. He put Gabby in the truck and helped to load the bags. Gabby and Karrington do not get to see each other as much due to Karrington's workload lately but she does approve of Rico. Gabby couldn't wait for Lillian and Morgan to meet him.

Rico gets in, puts his hand on her leg, and says, *"Baby, let's have a good weekend."*

Gabby smiled and leaned over to kiss Rico. She put her head on his shoulder and they went on their way.

NEW FRIENDS...
Everyone has made it to Lillian and Adam's and Lillian really had it laid out for her friends. It hasn't yet gotten hot and humid in New Orleans. It's a perfect overcast and breezy evening. After the guests come down from their rooms, they are met with waiters who serve them drinks. Lillian even employed Luna to usher everyone to their seats outside. Lillian gives everyone seat assignments so they can get to know each other. Rico is strategically seated between Lillian and Morgan who are ready to grill him. Everyone is getting to know each other and eating. Luna is making the rounds as she was just a toddler the last time everyone saw her!

Adam gets up and addresses the group. *"I would like to welcome all of you to New Orleans and the Lovelace home. I'm so proud of my wife."* He looks at her with love. *"She has created a great body of work. Thank you all for being here to celebrate her."*

Lillian is smiling as she sits and listens to Adam. She is described by her friends as the one in the group who dances to the beat of her own drum. Even after going to A&M, she found the coolest white guy in New Orleans who has her living in her soft era. Adam lets the guys know they will be having whiskey and cigars at the gazebo tonight because the girls are going out.

Lillian gets up just as Luna grabs her hands. *"Okay, ladies. Let's get ready. I'm going to get Luna ready for bed. We can leave around eleven."*

The couples go to their rooms to relax for a bit. Luna's voice carries as she asks her mom all types of questions before bed until Lillian says a firm 'good night' and tucks her in.

When ready to head out, Lillian gives Adam strict orders to not forget to check on her baby. He nods. The ladies look beautiful. They come down the stairs confidently as if they are on a runway. They say goodbye to their men and make their exit.

Once Adam has checked on Luna, he goes into the backyard where the guys have gathered. *"Finally, fellas,"* he yells.

The guys laugh and take their seats. A service crew has been hired to attend to the gentlemen for the night. As the guys settle into their cigars and drinks and start talking, they realize that they have much in common. As they get close to putting their cigars out, Rico stands up and the others become quiet.

He says, *"Thank you, Adam, for welcoming us into the Lovelace home. I want to give Gabby a surprise before we all leave. These ladies are her life and I want to propose to her while her girls are together. That would mean so much to her. I already have her mom's permission and I hope I have the other ladies' permission as well."*

The guys congratulated Rico. *"Let me know if you need anything. How are you going to do it,"* Adam asked.

Rico said, *"I was thinking about doing it after the play."*

Adam's face changed. *"No. That's Lill's night. How 'bout I get us a little corner at Doris Metropolitan. It's one of the most beautiful restaurants in New Orleans and then Gabby can have her own night."*

Rico agreed and it was settled. A couple of hours later, the ladies were coming in. They joined the men outside and talked about their night before everyone went to bed.

NEW BEGINNINGS...

The day of the play has arrived. Lillian is nervous but excited. Adam wakes up to her on the phone. From what he is hearing, she is either having a meeting or bossing someone around. *"Baby, what is going on? You should not be this stressed, you got this. Come back to bed, now."*

Lillian was more than a little stressed. When Adam asked her back to bed, she did not hesitate. It was just what she needed. Adam is attentive to her needs and she becomes more stress-free with each stroke, caress, and kiss. She is trying to be quiet and knowing that there are guests in the house but it's impossible to when it seems Adam is sucking the stress and anxiety out of her. As she feels her satisfaction approaching, she releases all that she is stressed about.

Lillian is lured out of a state of relaxation by the smell of bacon. She can hear Luna downstairs in the kitchen helping Morgan who has started breakfast. Amir is supporting her from the island on his laptop. Karrington and Dominique have gone for a run while Gabby and Rico are still in bed. Lillian can hear Adam getting in the shower so she goes to join him.

By the time they go downstairs to join everyone, Morgan has finished breakfast. Karrington and Dominique have made it back from their run. Everyone sits down to breakfast. The conversation centered on their respective evenings. The ladies were on Bourbon Street hanging out and they had dinner. When the guys were asked about their evening, they froze and looked at each other.

"What is happening right now? What did y'all do last night?" Karrington asked.

"We were planning a dinner for you all tomorrow before everyone leaves. There. You got the secret out of us," Adam said jokingly.

The ladies accepted that response, as did Rico. Lillian excused herself to get ready to go to the theater and prepare for the evening. She puts Morgan in charge of getting Luna ready. She kissed Adam and Luna goodbye and left for the theater.

. . . .

Everyone made it out to support Lillian. Her play was fantastic! Luna gave her flowers after the curtain call. The group went to dinner to celebrate Lillian's success. A member of the audience happened to be sitting at the table next to them. He greeted the group and asked Lillian if she was the director of tonight's play.

"I am," Lillian answered confidently.

"Would you like to work on a Broadway show?"

"Are you serious? Yes!" Lillian's eyes were wide with shock. Her friends and husband cheered. She looked at Adam who was smiling from ear to ear. She had his blessing.

Adam reached over and said, *"We're going to figure this out. I'm so proud of you!"*

Luna gave her mom a big kiss. *"Mommy, you are the best. I love you!"*

Lillian's mom kissed her on her cheek and said, *"I'm so proud of you, baby."* She's called Lillian her "baby" all her life.

Lillian started to tear up. Her dreams were coming true right before her eyes and her loved ones were present to share the moment with her. This night was perfect.

GABBY'S NIGHT

The next day is Gabby's day and the most beautiful thing about this evening, the men all decided not to tell their ladies because they know how they are. Rico and Adam were going out to prepare for the proposal and he told the ladies they were going out to get cigars for when they return tonight. Adam knew that Lillian or any of them didn't care when they got together. This was the perfect time to leave. Dominique had gone out for a run and Amir was in Adam's office working.

Lillian asked, *"How long will you all be gone?"*

Adam walked to her and kissed her forehead. *"We'll be back in about an hour."*

Rico gave Gabby a kiss and the men left. The ladies continued with their conversation. It's like the men knew it was time to leave. As soon as they were out of the way, the ladies began trading stories. Gabby started it off. She knew Karrington had been good all weekend, but she looked a little stressed.

"So, Karri, what's going on? You're the only one who seems a bit off this weekend. What's going on? Is everything good with work? Dominique?"

Karrington's friends know her better than anyone else, so she just came clean. *"Dominique and I are great at work. He is a beast and I love that about him. I've told you all about him and his lifestyle. I'm good with it because he makes my body sing,"* she said with a blush. *"But he's changed and working with him is becoming challenging."*

The ladies were quiet and looked to Gabby to continue the interrogation. Gabby obliged. *"Well, what are you thinking? Do you still want to be with him? How long does he have?"*

All the ladies laughed. Karrington runs when things get too real or if she can't figure it out. Through her smile, Karrington responded. *"I love Dom, but I can't. I love my job and I love being the best lawyer I can be. Working with him is both good and bad. I want to be comfortable where I'm working and I don't want to walk on eggshells wondering if someone is going to decipher a stare or a smile. I don't know if I just need to leave the office or leave him and stay at the office."*

Lillian said, *"I know what you went through with Jonathan. I know you're still trying to heal but Gabby did tell you to take it slow and you didn't. Now you have been tied up and tangled up in his web and now he's in love with you 'cause 'you are his everything.'"* Lillian all but rolled her eyes as she made finger quotes in the air.

Karrington knew Lillian was right. *"I'm going to have a conversation with him when we get back home. But I'm going to do the best thing for me. I'm not at the top of my list, Dom's feelings are."*

The ladies nodded in agreement. Karrington looked sad, but she was happy to be here with her friends and talk this out with them. Over an hour had passed and the guys were returning, and they were excited to go to dinner tonight before everyone prepared to leave the next day.

Lillian has made it home from the mall with her mom and Luna, and everyone is getting dressed for dinner tonight. Adam has finished getting dressed and he's out of Lillian's way. Gabby looks beautiful white sundress and Rico looks dapper in slacks and a white dress shirt. Gabby compliments him, she rarely sees him out of uniform dressed up. She has no idea this night is for her. Karrington is in a blue off-the-shoulder dress and Dominique is wearing a blue dress shirt and jeans. She usually tries to dress in Dominique's favorite color when they go out, tonight is no different.

She grabs her bag on their way out and turns and says, *"Dom, when we get back home, we need to talk. I love you, and I always want to be honest with you so there are some things we need to work out, where I am concerned."*

Dominique listened to her with intensity and answered, *"Okay. I'm sure whatever it is we can work it out."* They kissed and walked out of the room. Dominique didn't seem phased but he was a little worried. Morgan, Amir, Gabby, Rico, Karrington, Dominique, and Adam were downstairs waiting for Lillian.

Adam yells out, *"Let's go, baby."*

Lillian went to check on Luna and her mom. On her way, she yells, *"Here I come!"* They headed out to enjoy their final night together.

They make it to Doris Metropolitan and instantly fall in love with the top-notch scene. Earlier that day Adam had taken Rico to help him prepare for the evening and they were quickly ushered to their private dining room. The room was dimly lit and there were menus personalized for each couple. The men had successfully created a great night for the ladies. The ladies were impressed by the level of detail and planning that was done. The wine was served first — it was each lady's favorite. The entrees were up next. Karrington, the consummate seafood lover, was served a dish with lobster and crab. Gabby received the most succulent steak. Morgan had a delicious shrimp pasta with wine sauce and Lillian got her favorite chicken dinner. The men had the dish that was their lady's favorite. The dessert course was no different except Gabby didn't get one.

She turned to Rico with a quizzical expression. *"Rico, you don't know my favorite dessert?"*

Rico appeared shocked. *"I'll be right back. Let me check with the waiter."*

Gabby and the girls were confused but Karrington was upset. *"Gabby, how could he forget about your dessert?"*

Gabby was calm and remained quiet. A few minutes later Rico came back with a plate carrying a small silver dome.

Rico sat down. *"Gabby, you are sweeter than any dessert and you are special."*

Karrington, Lillian, and Morgan looked at each other with wide eyes as they realized what was taking place.

Rico continued. *"I know that your friends are aware of what you have been through. I know they are going to be there for you. I want to be here too...forever."*

Gabby let out a shaky breath. Tears well up in her eyes and she could hear her friends sniffling.

Rico lifted the dome lid to reveal a blue Tiffany box on the plate. He opened it and said, *"Gabrielle, would you please allow me to be your everything today, tomorrow, and forever?"*

Gabby could see the love in Rico's eyes. *"Yes, Rico. Yes!"*

The room cheered. Rico picked Gabby up and kissed her sweetly. Gabby's friends were truly happy for her.

Though happy for Gabby, Karrington had her conversation with Dominique on her mind. Their circumstance now seems more pressing in light of her friend's engagement. She is happy with Dominique but is it enough?

The couples happily leave the restaurant and head back to Lillian's. Adam planned a night out for the guys. He knew that the girls were going to want to spend this night with each other. The guys changed and kissed their ladies goodbye as they headed out for the evening.

The ladies were in the pajamas that Lillian had brought for them. Lillian and the girls laughed, cried, drank, and celebrated. They have a wedding to plan!

42

CHAPTER 5

The Perfect Petal

THE PAST

Karrington and Dominique have returned from a wonderful trip in New Orleans and it was time to get back to work. Dominique went in so it didn't seem suspicious that he and Karrington were out at the same time, and they returned on the same day. Karrington took off an additional two days. This is one of the things she wants to discuss with Dominique. While they were in New Orleans, the fact that they could go to a restaurant and kiss and hold hands and just enjoy themselves as a couple and now that they are back it's back to the same song and dance as if they are sneaking around and Karrington doesn't want that, but as she is organizing her thoughts for Dominique, they were interrupted by a phone call. She picks up the phone and almost drops it. *"No fucking way!"* she yells.

Karrington answers and you can hear the hesitation in her voice as she speaks, *"H-h-hello?"* It was as if it were a ghost on the other end.

Then her past speaks and her heart shatters. *"Hello, Karrington. I know you were not expecting to hear from me."*

Karrington covered her mouth as tears fell down her face. She could not believe she was hearing his voice after two years of no contact. *"Jonathan, what...what is it?"* she finally asked after she found her voice. Immediately, the memories of how he had treated her rushed to the surface and her anger rose. *"Why are you calling me? What do you want?"*

Jonathan cleared his throat and said, *"I'm glad you asked that. My mom passed away and I just thought you would want to know."*

Somehow, Karrington went up another gear in her anger. She recalled how his mother had treated her and the words his mom had spat at her the night she left for good. All too well, Karrington remembers being devastated. The way the love of her life had discarded her like trash and his mother was there to put the lid on top, she was fuming.

She gathered herself, but how she loved Jonathan came over her and she had to speak. *"Sorry for your loss. I'm sure you have all the support you need. Thanks for calling to let me know."* She started to hang up but heard him say something. She put the phone back to her ear. *"What did you say?"*

Jonathan repeated, *"Karrington, Mich—"*

Karrington cut him off. *"Don't you dare say Miss Grocery Store's name to me! Are you fucking kidding me? You think you are about to talk to me about your check-out girl?"* Karrington yelled.

Karrington could hear him trying to calm her down, but he knew her, and he knew that wasn't going to happen, but he continued, *"We're not together. I just thought you'd want to know about my mom and I wanted to know if you wanted to come to the funeral since she was your mother-in-law."*

Karrington could not believe what she was hearing. *"Jonathan if you don't get your ass off of my phone and how the fuck did you get my number anyway?"* Karrington was beyond furious. She began to think about where he could have gotten the number because she knew her family or close friends would never give it out.

"Karri, I got it from your job here at the law office."

Karrington yelled out she was going to sue them. Then she slowed down, took some deep breaths, and focused all her emotions into her last words to Jonathan. *"Listen to me carefully Mr. Jonathan Noah Thomas. Do not ever call me. Ever. I don't care what happens in your family. You have called and interrupted my day, my spirit, and my walk with God. Do not call me again."*

Karrington's tone was calm and clear and although it's been a minute, Jonathan knew what the tone meant. He also knew that this would be the last time he would ever speak to her.

Karrington is a wonderful giving woman but as soft as her heart is, her head never steers her wrong. She hung up and fell onto the couch. She lost track of time but when the doorbell rang she knew it was Dominique at the door. *Oh shit, that's Dom...perfect timing.* She let him in. Although he had no idea what she had been through, her face communicated what she needed and he obliged.

Dominique walked inside, turned, and locked the door. When he turned back around to greet Karrington, she was halfway to her room. He watched as her shirt fell to the floor. Her hips sashayed from side to side as she disappeared into her bedroom. Seconds later he heard the shower and removed his clothing on cue. He headed towards the shower, pausing momentarily when he entered the bathroom to watch her silhouette.

Karringston's hair draped over her shoulders and grew wavier with each drop of water. Dominique stepped in behind her and slid his arms around her waist. Karrington turned and faced him, and he noticed that she wasn't herself. Karrington was crying, Dominique could see her tears through the water that cascaded over her face.

"What's wrong?" Dominique asked, hoping he could help.

Karrington couldn't stop crying. Dominique turned the water off and got out of the shower then turned around with a towel for Karrington. He walked her to the bed, picked her up, and set her down. Dominique asked her to tell him what's wrong and she told him about the phone call she had just received from her ex-husband.

When Karrington explained everything to Dominic he got in bed and held her in his arms, and she cried herself to sleep. Dominic was furious. He felt helpless because he wasn't there. There's nothing that he could do at this moment. When Karrington woke up, he was right there.

"Karri, do you need anything?"

When he called her 'Karri' she knew that he was really being attentive and wanted to help. At this time, she wasn't ready to tell him everything, she needed him now more than ever. After the conversation with Jonathan, she simply wanted to forget the whole ordeal and just lay there with Dominique. He came from the kitchen with a glass of water and placed it on her side of the bed.

Karrington looks up at Dominique and says, *"Level 4 please, Sir."*

Dominique quickly begins and he carefully brings her limp body close to him. He caresses her body then goes to get oil and covers her body in oil and love licks. Dominique drinks from her and allows her to release each orgasm that she has.

When this level is requested from Karrington, Dominique instructs her to speak as she eases into her pleasure. *"Pretty Girl, I'm thirsty and I am ready to drink but I'm ready to hear what is wrong before we finish."*

Karrington hasn't been to this level in a while, but it was necessary. Dominique's instructions work for her mind, body, and soul. Karrington has been waiting for this moment for the last hour and a half.

Dominique positioned himself at her center and could feel that she was about to release. Dominique knows her body and he can feel that her pleasure is about to peak, and he slowly lifts his head and says very softly, *"Speak."*

Karrington's voice is shaky and barely above a whisper and she began to tell him what warranted this session. *"I got a phone call from my ex-husband today. He wanted to tell me about his mother and—"* Karrington was almost there and this moment took her breath away.

Dominique could taste that she was almost there. He continued to bring her to the end of the reason a Level 4 was requested. *"He wanted to tell me why he and the woman who he cheated on me with were no longer—"*

Right before she could finish her statement, Dominique commanded her to give him her pleasure.

Finishing in a scream, Karrington let out, *"TOGETHER!"*

With that, her body went limp again. She was finally able to ride the waves of her orgasm but this time, she released her anger and frustration at Jonathan as well.

Dominique gave Karrington her water and began to rub her gently again.

Karrington looked at him. *"That was the worst part of my day, but it's over now. Thank you."*

After Karrington regained consensus, Dominique cleaned up and got in bed. Then he asked, *"So he just called you out of nowhere? How did he get your number?"*

Karrington explained that he got her number from her old job. They needed her new information to continue to work with her replacement on a case she had been working on before she left. They continued to talk about the phone call and with each second of their conversation Karrington felt better. They talked until they fell asleep.

The next morning Dominique gets up and starts getting ready for work. Karrington has one more free day before she's due back at the office so she remained in bed.

While Dominique was getting dressed, she asked, *"Didn't you enjoy how we were in New Orleans? We went to dinner, went running in the morning, and I didn't feel like a* secret. *I loved being with you like that. Didn't you love that?"*

"I did. It's so easy being with you." He sat by her and continued. *"That was nice and I really enjoyed that too. Life with you is beautiful but it may take a little bit longer."* He kissed her on her forehead and went into the bathroom.

Karrington watched him groom himself and responded matter-of-factly, *"I don't have a little bit."*

He turned and saw that her face was serious. Dominique recognized this face. This was Karrington in the courtroom. He finished in the bathroom and took her hand so she could walk him to the door, and he promised to come back after work to continue their conversation. He leaned down and kissed her goodbye.

Karrington moved away from him. *"After the conversation with Jonathan yesterday, I realize I can't let people use me as a placeholder until they need me. Jonathan calling me yesterday was a violation and I don't want you to follow in his footsteps. When you come back tonight, I need you to have a solution for us. Have a good day."*

She planted a kiss on his lips and closed the door. Karrington was not stressed because the ball was in Dom's court. She put on a pot of coffee and took a shower. After getting dressed and fetching her coffee, she went home to Morgantown to spend the day with her parents.

THE PRESENT

On his way to work, Dominique replayed Karrington's words in his head. She was right and he felt she was the right woman for him. He thought about how he felt when he first saw her. *Karrington Rose is my person. There is no other woman I want to be with 'cause no other woman will be like her.* Dominique is very organized and his thoughts for

Karrington are no different. Dominique had some serious decisions to make.

He pulled into his parking space and tried to get in the frame of mind for work, but he feared these thoughts would be with him all day. Dominique went in for his morning brief. Although he was leading the teams, his mind was on Karrington. He agreed with what she had said about New Orleans. That was one of the best times they have had since they began seeing each other. He took a break and called his best friend. He doesn't trust many people but Colin has been with Dominique through a lot of highs and lows.

"What's up, frat," Colin answered.

Dominique made small talk for as long as he could.

Colin could tell something was off. Being his usual blunt self, he called him out. *"What is going on?"*

Dominique came clean. *"Man, I've been dreading this day, but Karrington brought up a conversation to me this morning. I'm going to have to make some decisions about our personal relationship and our work relationship. We were in New Orleans this past weekend and we had the best time. She mentioned this morning how great it was to just be able to hang out together and be out as a couple. Man, because we work together it feels like we creep around like we're cheating on the job and she doesn't deserve that. I really don't know what to do."*

Colin is always so straight up with Dominique and this time is no different than any other. *"Frat, you are going to have to make a choice. You can be exclusive with your woman because she is all yours...and you haven't had this in a long time. You could also end the personal shit and continue to work with her, you've just got to decide what is going to make you guys happy? Do you want to let the office know or just be coworkers? You all have been professional to this point, but you've got to decide what is going to make both of you happy, I'm sure you are overthinking this."*

Dominique switched his attention from the door and began to focus completely on his date and the words coming out of her mouth.

Continuing, she said, *"I think we should just focus on our work relationship and see if it's the passion that we have for each other or if we really can't be without each other."*

He took a sip of water as he processed her words. She could see the disappointment in his eyes. In a low voice, he replied, *"Karrington, are we breaking up? I respect your decision but it is not what I want."*

She squeezed his hands gently and leaned in. Dominique met her lips right before the main course. They continued to talk about the changes in their relationship. When they were finished, they went back to Karrington's place so she could pack a few things to spend the night at Dominique's.

They made love to each other intensely. This was their way of saying goodbye — for now. When they woke up the next morning for work, Karrington knew the play. She hung back to ensure that she didn't arrive too closely behind him. It was as if this underscored the importance of her decision. She said to herself, *I can't go on like this anymore. Ending it was the right decision.*

FUTURE

It's been six months since Karrington and Dominique decided to pause their relationship. Gabby was preparing for her wedding so the girls would come together to celebrate. Karrington is settling nicely into her new firm while Dominique travels back and forth to see his parents in Liberty.

The last six months have been an emotional roller coaster. They have kept in touch — probably they always will. She would call him about cases she was working on to get his advice and he would do the same. They had a connection that was not easily broken. Though the time apart has been difficult for them both, it was exactly what Karrington needed. She was trying to detox from their relationship.

After she had pointed out what was missing in their relationship, it was clear that Dominique was not comfortable being exclusive with her. While she appreciated his position knowing how hard he had worked to be where he is, she wanted more. However, she would not want him to compromise everything he's worked so hard for. She did not want to force him to choose so she joined another firm as a partner. This was a good move. Dominique was more comfortable going out with her now but she didn't have much free time. She had to put in extra time to learn the ropes at her new job. Their relationship suffered despite their best efforts.

Dominique missed Karrington. They were apart more than they were together. His firm was still on top but when his father became ill, his mother needed help. He had to work remotely for two weeks a month. Thankfully, his formidable team kept going. This arrangement meant he saw less of Karrington which has helped to keep his mind off the split and helped him to cope with the separation.

The silver lining for him was that he and Karrington still talked often. He confided in her about his dad. She was his rock and they had always been there for each other, so when he called Karrington and asked her to come and see him, he needed his friend, she said yes and came for the weekend. Dominique's excitement was clear. She told him she would be in Liberty on Friday. When Dominique realized that she intended to drive, he told her he'd get her a plane ticket instead.

. . . .

Friday has arrived and Karrington has landed in Liberty. The bright smile on his face helped Karrington to spot him in the busy terminal. She threw her arms around him. Time stood still as they embraced. Dominique reached down to get her bags and they walked to the car.

She was not sure how she would feel when she saw him but she missed him. When she made it to the car, she couldn't hold it in any longer. *"I'm so happy to see you!"* she exclaimed.

He pulled her in for a deep kiss as if he was a dehydrated man discovering water after weeks in a desert. They kissed for what seemed like hours. After a while, she pulled back and said, "You still got it, Dom!"

They laughed and made their way to his parents' home. When they arrived, his mother met them at the door. *"Karri, baby come on in. Dominique, let her go so she can get in here."* Dominique's mother loved Karrington because her son was in love with her. *"Karri, I cooked all your favorites."*

Karrington loved Mrs. Jewel and Mr. Eli who was in the living room waiting to see her.

When she walked in, Mr. Eli said, *"Karri, it's so good to see you, baby. You make an old man happy."*

Dominique had taken Karrington to meet his parents early in their relationship. They had really taken to her and she loved them. When she found out Dominique's father wasn't well there was no way she was not going to see him. She really needed to get away. It also didn't hurt to see Dominique. It had been a while.

Karrington went over to hug him while Dominque took her things to the room where she would be staying. She sat on the couch and talked with Mr. Eli and Mrs. Jewel. Later that evening, they ate dinner together and Dominique's mom gave him a list of things that she needed for his dad.

Dominique and Karrington left and went to the store. This was the closest either of them had come to going on a date in a very long time. As they walked through the aisles looking for the items on his mom's list, Karrington asked nervously, *"So, Dom, are you dating anyone? I don't know if I really want to know but I'm still asking."*

Dominique looked at her quizzically, as he pushed the cart. His voice was calm and confident. *"Karrington, I am waiting for you."* With that, he stepped ahead of her.

Karrington was stunned and deep down she felt the same. They checked out and went back to Dominique's parents' home. After they returned and put the items away, Dominique returned to the living room to help his dad to bed.

On his way out, Mr. Eli turned to her wearing a solemn expression. *"Karrington, make an honest man out of my son. He loves you like I love my Jewel."*

She smiled and said, *"Wow, Mr. Eli. That's a lot of love."* She ran to him and kissed him on the cheek.

Dominique, trying unsuccessfully to hide his smile, continued to lead his father to rest. A few minutes later, he returned to the living room to find Karrington doing some work. *"So how is the new firm treating you? Are they working you too hard?"*

Karrington looked up from her laptop. Her hair was in a high bun. She had her black-frame glasses on, and rocking her pink and green pajamas. Dominique loved seeing her like this. She patted the cushion next to her for him to sit. With a wink, she said, *"Nothing I can't handle. I've had the best teacher so I got this."*

He leaned over and kissed her on her cheek.

She closed her laptop and said, *"I'm done. I'm all yours."*

Karrington asked Dominique, *"So what's going on in your world? I miss talking to you."* He and Karrington talked about their jobs and what was going on in their lives. Karrington asked Dominique if he wanted to go to Gabby's wedding with her next month.

He agreed. He had a great time in New Orleans with the guys and they have kept in touch since they left. *"How do you feel about what my dad said?"*

She looked at him and said, *"Are you serious?"*

Dominque nodded and searched her face for an answer.

She said, *"Dom, I love you, but I must be considered, and I deserve to be in a full relationship. What do you think about what he said?"* she asked him.

Dominique took her hands looked at her and said, *"The first time I saw you, I knew you were the woman for me, and you are still the woman for me."*

Karrington knew he meant it and the conversation was getting a bit heavy, so she put a pin in it. *"I'm going to bed. It's been a long day. I've got to help your mom tomorrow find a gift for one of her friends. I must be up early but I will sleep on what you are saying."* Karrington kissed Dom goodnight and went into the room.

MR. ELI

When Karrington woke up the next morning, she woke up to the sounds of a man crying. It was Dominique. Karrington jumped out of the bed and ran toward the cries. Dominique's father had passed away in his sleep. As she stood and watched Dominique take care of his mom, she knew she had to take care of him. Dominique turned to leave the room and saw Karrington. With long, desperate strides he walked to her. Falling to his knees, he wrapped his hands around her waist and sobbed. Karrington rubbed his face and stood there while waves of grief rocked his body.

When his shoulders relaxed, she raised his head to study his face. *"What do you need?"* she asked softly.

Karrington jumped right in and began to help. She knew that at this moment she was going to have to be strong for Dominique and Ms. Jewel. She called her coworkers and informed them that due to an emergency, she would be working remotely in the upcoming week. She assisted Dominique's mom as people were coming in to prepare Mr. Eli. Once that part was over, Dominique's mom sat quietly, while he called his siblings to let them know of their dad's passing. Karrington was right by Dominique's side, almost like his shadow.

Karrington went back home after the week with plans to return for the funeral on the weekend. Her friends wanted to be there for Dominique and support Karrington. Lillian, Morgan, and their families would also be there on Friday while Gabby and Rico would fly in on Saturday morning.

Karrington met all of Dominique's siblings and family and her friends gave him a lot of love. After the services and everyone went back home, Karrington stayed until Sunday. She and Dominique drove back to Fairmont while his sister stayed back to be with his mom for a while. On their way back home, Karrington talked to keep him engaged. As they got closer to Karrington's place, she told him she wanted him to spend the night with her. Dominique could only nod yes. He ended up staying with Karrington for a week while they continued to work remotely. Karrington took care of Dominique each day he was there. She cooked, made him go on walks with her, cried with him, and drove him to his place to get clothes. She also checked on his mom every day.

. . . .

A couple of months passed. Dominique's mom was still taking the loss hard. Her children continued to check on her every day, but he didn't like her being by herself. She had friends in Fairmont and since Dominique lived closer to her than his siblings, she agreed to move to a senior community near him so he could check on her and not worry.

With his father passing and his mom being alone, Dominique had some decisions to make, and those decisions included Karrington. He felt life was too short and he didn't want to waste another day not letting Karrington know how he felt. It was time for Gabby's wedding, and he and Karrington would be leaving for Morgantown in the morning. They decided to stay at Dominique's, as he was getting his mother together before they left for the wedding. Karrington told him she was going to her place to get a few things, and this was perfect because Dominique had a plan. He wanted to marry Karrington now more than ever.

Karrington had thrown clothes in a bag, she would sort it out when she got back, but she didn't like leaving Dominique alone. On her way back, she thought about how much she loved and cared for Dom and sharing her life with someone. She thought about being Mrs. McCullin but that would have to wait, her friend's big day comes first.

When she arrived at Dominique's, she thought it was strange he didn't come to meet her to get her bags from the car, so she left them and began walking to the door. When she opened the door, Dominique was standing in the living room in a tux!

"WHAT IS GOING ON, DOMINIQUE?!" Karrington was in shock. When she surveyed the room filled with candles, she knew.

Dominique began to speak. *"Karrington Danyell Rose, I am in love with you, and I want to spend the rest of my life with you. I love you and I want to give you the relationship you deserve. I will start by healing the wounds from your past. Then I will work on being the man you need. I just can't be without you, and I will spend the rest of my life making you happy. I keep saying 'my' because I'm going to give you everything you need while I'm here and if it's you who leaves before me, you accepting this proposal will fulfill me for the rest of my life because all I want is you. I love you Karrington. Please, will you marry me?"*

When she looked at Dominique down on one knee with a diamond that glistened in the candlelight, tears streamed down her face.

"Yes, I will! I will marry you, Dominique, and I will spend the rest of my life making you happy."

Dominique had already spoken to her parents and siblings, he had also called the girls, and he had everyone's blessings.

Dominique stood up and pulled Karrington close. He kissed her so gently as if she was a delicate flower that he didn't want to crush. She was so happy she didn't even realize she had on yoga pants, and as she was coming out of her stage of euphoria she could only laugh. They celebrated that night as only they could and the next day they got on the road to go and celebrate Gabby and Rico.

When Karrington and Dominique made it to her parents' home to get dressed for the wedding, her mom and dad were outside to greet them. Karrington's mom ran to her side of the car to get a glance at her ring.

"I'm going to have another son!" Karrington's dad yelled.

At that moment, Dominique began to sob. He hasn't heard a man call him 'son' since the night his dad died. Mr. Rose hugged him and there was no need for words. Dominique had a father again.

Fletcher hugged his daughter on her way into the house, he whispered to her, *"This is the one, Pudding. Daddy is not as worried about you now, but you know where I am."*

She nodded with tears in her eyes and kissed him on the cheek. Katherine and Fletcher were very overjoyed.

When the newly engaged couple arrived at the wedding, Karrington went to find the bride and get into her dress. She kissed her fiancé and off she went.

"CONGRATULATIONS!!!!" Lillian, Morgan, and Gabby greeted her as she entered the room. Karrington was so happy. Not only had all her friends found amazing men who loved them, but they were still close to each other.

Karrington zipped Gabby's dress and she asked, *"Are you ready?"*

Gabby looked at her and said, *"For the first time in my life, I am sure. Yes, I'm ready."* Gabby looked into her friend's eyes. *"Let him make you happy. It's ok."* They hugged and wiped each other's tears.

Gabby and Rico's wedding was beautiful and after everyone danced the night away, it was time for the new couple to leave for their honeymoon. Karrington and Lillian talked to Morgan about her upcoming wedding and the girls expressed excitement about Karrington's. When the night ended, Karrington and Dominique decided to drive the nineteen miles back to Fairmont. The last two days have been a whirlwind. They were just ready to be together.

Soon, after they made it back to Dominique's place, Karrington was wearing only her three-carat diamond ring. Dominique began at Level 1, taking it slow and easy on his soon-to-be wife. When he sensed that her climax was near, he peeled his mouth from her lips and in one fluid motion, he got up, lifted her, and placed her on top of him.

As she sank onto him, he whispered, *"You feel amazing."*

Guided by his skillful hands, Karrington looked Dominique in his eyes and whispered, *"This is perfect."*

About The Author

MILLICENT R. BAKER is a new fiction author who has now released book 3 of a 3 part series. She writes about love, romance, and pure happiness. Her stories focus on strong women who prioritize relationships as they work to overcome adversities. She is also a thriving social media influencer and entertainment blogger.

Millicent is a southern girl who graduated from Alabama A&M University and Ashford University. She is a proud member of Alpha Kappa Alpha Sorority who works tirelessly in her community. A woman of diverse interests and skills, she currently works in the nuclear power industry. She lives in Dallas, Texas with her daughter, Lillian.

Stay In Touch

**This is the third and final book of the Rose series.
So let's stay stay in touch!**

Website: Millichun.com

Email: millichun08management@gmail.com

TikTok: millichun08

Instagram: @millichun

YouTube: MillichunTV